I0626414

Captured by Christ
Copyright © 2025 by Kristy Benefield
All rights reserved

ISBN 979-8-9933129-0-3
Library of Congress Control Number 2025921076

All scripture references and/or quotations are taken from
The Holy Bible, New International Version®, NIV ®
Copyright © 1973, 1978, 1984, 2011 by Biblica, Inc.®

Suggested source for biblical context and/or commentary (not quoted or referenced)
Got Questions Ministries
Copyright © 2002-2025 All rights reserved
www.gotquestions.org
www.bibleref.com

Cover Art by Hannah Wheeler
Photography by Kristy Benefield

For my first,

Jesus

Inspired by my second,

Michael

Contents

The why behind the words

I like words and I love Jesus. I pray that my words help others find hope and healing in Him. I am a flawed, imperfect human and the daughter of a King. Let's start there. I feel that lending you a glimpse into my life will help you better understand the why behind my words, where the love of writing came from, and how Jesus and prayer saved my life.

Anxiety played a starring role in the script of my life. Fear was my companion. I have also been clinically diagnosed with obsessive compulsive disorder. At times, I fought these things with medication, but more often than not, I turned to alcohol. Even though I had a strong Christian foundation, most of my life I had one foot in and one foot out. There was a real tug of war at work from a very young age with a preacher grandfather and an alcoholic father. And by the time I was 44 years old, I was a full blown, high-functioning alcoholic. I did all the things you're supposed to do. I checked all the boxes from a societal point of view. As a wife and a mother, I got the "stuff" done. But the drinking, I can tell you, was every night and it was a lot. I convinced myself that the amount of alcohol I drank was totally fine and that it wasn't harming me or causing the anxiety, panic attacks, or intrusive thoughts, it was helping with them. "Drinking just takes the edge off". And that is the furthest thing from the truth.

> My anxiety and fear were fires, and the alcohol was the fuel
> I was dousing those fires with.
> I wasn't living, I was barely surviving, just hanging on.

On the last day I drank alcohol, the app that I used to send me a daily scripture, sent 1 Peter 5:8 "Be alert and of sober mind. Your enemy the devil prowls around like a roaring lion looking for someone to devour." (NIV) I read that scripture and it felt like God was saying, "Kristy, I didn't make you for this. I did not make you for drinking". I had received many other warnings or messages over my drinking years, but this felt different. It felt alarming. And how did I respond? I ignored it like I did all the others and finished that day out as I finished all my days out... with drinks.

My journey to sobriety was deliverance. My journey to healing why I drank was difficult, but necessary. God had been trying to get my attention for a long time and I could see that so clearly now. So many gentle whispers and nudge after nudge, I could feel Him calling me and I just chose not to listen. If things didn't happen the way they did, I honestly think I would still be drinking. I feel with all my heart, the circumstances had to be difficult for me to stop drinking for life. Understand that fully. I'm not referring to "life" as a length of time. I mean to keep my life, to go on living, I had to stop drinking. Now, here is where everything I went through is all worth it. And I can't mean this more. The re-introduction to Jesus I experienced is the truest, real. The realest truth.

A lot of pain and shame and guilt came with my eyes being opened. I had to face all the reasons why I drank; the pain I was avoiding from my childhood, self-medicating fear and anxiety, among other reasons, and it hurt. Plain and simple, it hurt! Healing hurts, but it is necessary pain that brings you to the other side of something you've experienced. I want to encourage you. If you live with pain like that, let me share, Jesus is willing and able to heal it. There was a great healing that came to me and this piece, right here, is the heart of my message.

I want you to consider the pain and the shame I felt from facing my past and how I had been living my life. How heavy it made me feel. These things have a physical weight to them, yes? Humans feel stress and pain physically. We carry burdens. And, I want you to focus on that because, I hope to help you capture something. There is a gravity that comes with facing past sin. It is heavy. Almost like toting around a backpack of pain bricks.

Now...multiply the weight I felt from my sin and shame by mankind!! That is the gravity of what hung on Jesus, as He hung on the cross. Does that resonate? Ever heard someone say, "the weight of the world"? Well, for Jesus, that was His reality. He wasn't just beaten beyond being barely recognizable as a man. He wasn't just spit on, mocked and humiliated, and had a crown of piercing thorns shoved onto the brow of His head. He carried the sin weight of the world, of mankind.

I can't write about Jesus and how I came to know Him, without sharing who He is and what He did. I don't want to assume that everyone who reads this book, calls Jesus their Savior. I hope that is the case, but I can't know that for sure. So here it is friend, I don't know where you stand with Jesus Christ, but He died for your sins, whether you believe in Him or not. There will be a real time in your life when you feel a stirring about this very notion. I hope you sit down inside it and see the truth inside. Because that is what's inside, truth. He is the truth. The profound privilege of simply knowing Jesus Christ has a richness and reward far beyond what this broken world can ever offer you with its fleeting allure. This world will never satisfy you.

For the believers that live in the reality that Jesus carried your sin on the cross with Him, I hope these words create a stirring in your soul that draws you to the center of God's heart. Psalm 139 says "more than the grains of sand are your thoughts for me". Grains of sand! Can you even fathom how many grains of sand are on earth? God's thoughts for you are MORE than that. Does that resonate? We aren't actually capable of fully grasping the love that encapsulates us from our Heavenly Father and His Son, Jesus, who gave His life for us.

As far as the pain of my past, and how Jesus brought me to a place of peace and healing, I want you to understand very clearly that God doesn't want you living a life of shame and guilt. He broke the chains of sin for you to have freedom from those emotions. God has given me the ability to look at my past, see all the ugly and feel gratitude that He rescued me from it, rather than shame because I lived it. That is what grace looks like. My past was bought and paid for long ago. He was with me in the midst of the darkness while I was drowning in alcohol and living in fear. He was also already in my future, waiting to embrace me with open arms and hold me after facing my giants.

He became the first person I wanted to talk to. So, my journey began with prayer. Prayer set the foundation for the peace I live in today. When my mind began spinning false scenarios and fear started to creep in, I would fight back with prayers of praise. I handed everything to Him and followed it with praise. Anxiety flees worship of the Lord. Consistently turning to God in prayer developed a deep relationship and longing to know Him more, which led me to scripture. Reading the Bible draws me closer to Him and opens a world of words that come to me. Random words that jump out at me or get repeated. So, I write them down.

At the start of 2025, I decided to pick one day a week devoted to writing and fasting. I happen to love the book of Psalms, so I decided that I would take a shot at writing one. I had no idea where it would lead. What I found is that writing, for me, has become a place that I go to rather than something I do. It is a place of retreat where I meet the Lord. I pray and talk to Him as I write. I ask Him to meet me in my words, and He does. It almost feels as if I am stepping over a threshold and into a quiet renewal where it is only Him and me. I began to share some of the things I wrote and kept being told to share more. Through prayer and the confirmation of others, I felt led to create this study. As I write this introduction, I am still on this journey with Him and honestly, my hope is to write with Him all the days of my life.

I didn't FIND Jesus. He's never been missing.
He wasn't lost. I was. I found my identity in Him.

By His words, I am fed. And it is through words that I express my love and gratitude to Him. He has captivated my mind and captured my heart.
I am forever His.

Daily Work

READ
Read the psalm/ prayer writing.

STUDY
Study each scripture reference that accompanies the writing. Where do you see each scripture in the writing? Which scripture(s) capture your attention? Commit one to memory. Place it where you will read it several times a day; phone lock screen, Post-it notes, dash of your car. There are many sources for deeper scripture meaning and context. I like BibleRef.com and GotQuestions.org for context and additional biblical commentary. They both offer apps to download.

RESPOND
Respond to the prompting questions for deeper connection to God's word and observe what thoughts and emotions arise.

PRAY
Pray for God to meet you in this time of reflection. You will receive prompts throughout your study. Lean into them.
Pray with anticipation of God's response.
James 4:8 says draw near to God and He will draw near to you.

POUR
Write your own psalm/prayer or short story to record what God has revealed. Pour out your heart and thoughts on paper. Depending on your season, this may be praise, this may be Spirit led conviction, or intense request. The point of this exercise is to address what surfaces, write it down, and consider sharing your words. Suggestion: I wrote with scripture in mind. Prayer and the Holy Spirit brought words and topics to the forefront, which led me to specific scriptures.

Small Group Option
This study can be done on your own or within a small group setting. Your words and thoughts can bring light and life to others, so don't be afraid to invite others on this journey and share your words and prayers with each other. Scripture tells us the importance of fellowship and how valuable our time with each other is. "As iron sharpens iron, so one person sharpens another." (Proverbs 27:17)

Suggestions for getting the most out of this study...

Scripture

Physically pick up your Bible whenever you can for reading scripture. Try to avoid using your phone or tablet if possible. Reading a physical copy of the Bible is sensory. You can feel the weight of the Word as you hold the entire, complete work in your hands. You can hear the sound of the pages wrestling as your fingertips shuffle to a specific chapter or verse. Your eyes are engaged as the Word and the Holy Spirit, at work, capture your attention and lift words right off the page speaking directly to you. Have you ever held it to your face and took a deep breath? Smell the printed pages of the gospel. Reading the Bible can be a very personal, physically experiential activity. The author of the Bible is also the author of your story. Join Him in writing it. This is what leads to our next topic... Prayer.

Prayer

Find your secret place and your prayer rhythm. Create an environment that almost feels like you're stepping into a location, for One on one time with the Father, Son and Holy Spirit. This could be a quiet walk where you are undistracted by headphones and focused on deep conversation with God, allowing the symphony and beauty of His creation be the backdrop. This could be just as Jesus instructed, in a room, with the door closed. (Matthew 6:6-7) The place you pray doesn't have to be a secret place, the secret will be you stepping into an unseen prayer room that is only yours and His. Follow the prayer example of Christ... Matthew 14:23, Mark 1:35 & Luke 5:16

Writing with Reverence

One thing I always do when I am writing, is capitalize the pronouns of God, our Father, Jesus, and the Holy Spirit. Whenever I am referring to myself, I use lowercase letters. I started doing this from the very beginning of my writing journey and it has stuck. I even use this practice when I am texting with friends about Him, or journaling in a notebook. I want to approach the throne of grace with humility and hope that even capitalization choice can bring honor to God. Lastly, notice your emotions when you write to and about God. They will change. Ask God to speak into them through your words. Don't hold back. He sees it all, however you can honor Him by acknowledging that He can, in fact see it all. Expose your heart, hide nothing.

Rhythm

Routine and structure help keep my soul well. Don't misunderstand my statement. Relationship with Jesus Christ keeps my soul well. But I keep my relationship with Him at the forefront of my life, by creating time and space for Him throughout my entire day. Intentional time in prayer, fasting, studying God's word, and fellowship are important to me, and they are all built into my schedule. Set out to create a rhythm with the Lord and ask Him to help you sustain it. Of course, there will be interruptions and disturbances to this schedule, but you will find that the time you spend in regular communion with God, help carry you through the times of disturbance.

Timing

This study can take 30 days or 30 weeks. The Daily Work section lays out the process of this study, but the timing is really yours to design. You will find what timing works best for you, but don't rush it. Pray through it and ask God to meet you each time you start.

Fasting & Emotions

As you read in the brief bio, I chose to fast as part of a one year journey. This too, is something you can make your own. I chose one day a week to fast for a 24 hour period. I chose to fast on the day I intended to write a prayer or psalm. I want to remind you to give yourself some grace here. There were days I went 24 hours and days I only made it 20. Some days were definitely harder than others. This is a heart posture focus, not a focus on length of time. Notice your emotions as you study, pray and when you write to and about God. They will change. I experienced a variety of emotions during this time. Because I chose to fast on these days, I noticed my hunger, which I brought to Him. I wrote when I felt like it and when I didn't. What I found is that God would meet me inside each of those feelings and moods, which helped me put them to paper and sort through what had Kingdom value, what needed exposing and what needed comforted. His words fed my soul and spoke into my feelings.

01.

Breathe You In

You are my resting place.
You loosen the grip anxiety has on me.
i see a place in my heart where i can find refuge and gain strength.
That place is You.
You are hidden in my heart but not hiding from me.
That is our secret place.
You are a place and a love that i can't describe with words.
i can try to find them, but i am not sure words that beautiful exist.
The closest i can get is Holy.
To abide in You is absolute comfort.
To know Your love, is to know total peace.
Your love is an ever-unfolding gift.
i can never reach the center of it.
Your love encapsulates me and covers me.
i can quickly remove dark whispers by saying Your name.
i have seen the power in Your name.
i dream about it.
i use Your name for protection.
Your name is a place where i can rest.
i can take a walk and feel You grip my hand,
as the wind blows through my fingers.
Let's walk together always.

There is no place i can go, and You aren't there.
There is no place i ever want to go without You.
The habits and worry of yesterday no longer have any power.
They can't be used as weapons any longer.
They try to speak over my life,
but their noise is drowned out by the sound of Your quiet stillness.
How did i miss You for so long?
What was i waiting for?
i'm sorry for my delay.
You are the greatest treasure buried in my heart.
Jesus, i am Yours, call me Yours.
i love You.
When i get out of the shadow of my own way,
Your light is so splendid and radiant to step into.
The light to my path is You walking in front of me.
i want to follow You so closely, should You stop walking,
my face would collide with Your back.
i would wrap my arms around You and breathe You in.
To be near You is gratitude.
Near You is where i always want to be.

Scripture References
Psalm 37:7
Proverbs 18:10
2 Corinthians 10:5
Philippians 4:6-7
James 4:7
Psalm 119:105

Scripture Study & Questions

Read each of the scriptures that were referenced after the writing.
Are you able to locate them in the writing? As you go through each week of this study, try to focus on how scripture speaks directly to you. Whenever you write something, do it with scripture in mind. Try to engage your mind, keeping the Word of God active and up front. Compare everything to God's Word, as we know it is a useful tool. (2 Timothy 3:16)

Q1 Of the referenced scriptures, which one(s) leapt off the page and grabbed your attention? What particular words/ phrase stood out?

_____

_____

_____

_____

_____

Q2 Where is the first place you turn when experiencing fear or worry? Do you isolate? Do you turn to friends or family? Do you turn it over to God in prayer?

_____

_____

_____

_____

_____

Q3 With the many times man is told not to fear, in the Bible, why do you think it is so hard to follow this command, and be assured by the repeated promise that He will never leave, nor forsake us?

_____

_____

_____

_____

Words Come

Before you write anything, survey your heart and mind. What words come to mind? What emotions surface? Pray for God to give you words that reveal more about these feelings and ask Him to examine them.
Notice what is He laying on your heart. Unless you are overwhelmed with words, try to give this exercise at least 24-48 hours.
Let the words come and write them here.

Now it is your turn. Take the words above and express them in a prayer, psalm or short story. The moment you sit down to write, pray "meet me here, Lord."
If you are an artist, paint or draw an expression of these words or emotions revealed to you during this time of reflection.

02.

In The Garden

You don't place people in Hell.
People separate themselves from You, which is hell.
You called my name repeatedly.
i didn't listen.
Again and again, You called.
Sin after sin, i remained unresponsive.
The enemy foothold became a gaping wide open opportunity.
A very dark cloud formed over my life.
The final straw broke.
i broke.
i ended up on my knees in desperate, trembling fear.
Fear so consuming, i didn't know how i could go on.
Fear so encompassing and unrelenting that i felt my end coming.
It was the darkest dark.
The blackest abyss.
The loneliest silence.
It felt like You blinked.
A blink is a period of time, without You, that feels like an eternity.
i know what running from You looks like.
i know what chasing nothing looks like.
i saw only a moment of what an existence without You looks like.
No, never again.
Don't ever blink at me again, God.
i know Your hand remained on me, You don't abandon.
i perceived that You lifted just one finger off of me.
"This is what it looks like without Me."
It was excruciating.
Never again.
You have my attention
The cycle is broken.
Life is linear again.
And Heaven is on the horizon.

You are the great dawn of light, bursting forth,
annihilating the darkness.
Shadow flees from You.
You are the outstretched arms as this prodigal runs home.
Jesus, You are the outstretched arms on the cross, crushing my sin.
In every way that I battle with my flesh, You did also.
You don't leave me in times of trouble, You are my example.
With my knees and my face pressed against the floor,
i begged for relief.
"Come quickly, Lord, i can bear this no longer."
i consider my Lord, in the garden, praying with trembling fear.
Fear so great, His body sweat blood.
The fear He faced would be my rescue.
my sin brought Jesus to the garden and put Him on His knees.
He was praying to have the Father remove
the atonement of my sin from before Him.
His death was my deliverance.
Oh Jesus, why?
Why?
Two thousand years later, after the most inexplicable display of love,
You didn't leave me on my knees.
You picked me up, placed Your hand under my chin
and pulled me close enough to whisper "because I love you."
i love You back!
Can You hear me?
Jesus, i love You back!
Can You feel my soul crying out in immense gratitude?

You pulled me from darkness.
You are my rescue.
i can't be without You.
Without relent, in my entirety, i yearn for You.
Be in all of my moments.
Remain in me, as i remain ever seeking You.

Scripture References
Psalm 38
Psalm 18:4-6
Psalm 34:4
Luke 15:11-32
Hebrews 4:15
Matthew 26:36-46
Mark 14:32-42
Luke 22:41-44

Scripture Study & Questions

While reading the scriptures referenced for this writing, slow down and read with intention. Take the time to reflect on the emotional and physical experience of Jesus praying in the garden, as expressed in the gospels. Imagine the skin of His knees pressed against the garden soil. Can you see His tear drops puddled on the ground just beneath His face as He pray?

Q1 God's "no" to Jesus in the garden, was our "yes" to forgiveness and eternity with Him. Jesus willingly and joyfully went to the cross for us after that "no". How does your heart and mind respond to this gift?

_____

_____

_____

_____

_____

Q2 From the writing, you clearly see fear and what felt like a real and present danger expressed. Describe a time when you have been overwhelmed with fear. How did you respond? How did relief come?

_____

_____

_____

_____

Q3 It is a scientific fact that anxiety flees from praise. God intended for us to experience freedom, not fear. How can you implement a practice of praise prayer for fear removal? How will you apply God's Word to send fear away?

_____

_____

_____

_____

_____

Words Come

Give me ears to hear, Lord.

Bring life to these words.

03.

Rise & Smile

When i wake, You are already there, smiling at me.
The sun has come up with all its glorious radiance created by You.
i rested last night....oh, thank You.
Whether i sleep well or not, i still have You.
And that alone, gives my heart rest.
i have air in my lungs this morning.
i hear birds singing Your praise outside.
They sing songs for You and i enjoy their sweet melodies.
You share everything.
Before i leave the place i lay my head,
i have more blessings that i can count.
Help me to begin and end in gratitude.
Let me start and finish with You on my mind.
Waking to the simple truth that Jesus is my Savior is the sweetest
morning blessing.
Then others come pouring in.
They flood me.
Blessings innumerable.

Forgive me when i rise and don't acknowledge them.
i don't want to rush out of slumber and out the door,
without sending You a good morning love note.
Your glory and presence are always there.
How could i possibly skip over it?
And somehow, sometimes, i do.
You are without shadow, without variation.
The only variation in You are the many ways You show Your love.
i love Your smile, Lord.
i see it everywhere.
i delight in Your delight.
You make me smile.
To smile upon waking is to have true peace that Jesus Christ is mine.
And i am His.
Don't go anywhere, stay right here.

Scripture References
Lamentations 3:22-23
Psalm 139:17-18
Hebrews 1:3
Ephesians 3:20-21
James 1:17
Psalm 37:4

Scripture Study & Questions

Scripture, through the Holy Spirit, comes to life in the eyes of the reader.
It can change each time you read it, confirming that it is alive and active.
Scripture becomes part of you and implants itself into your heart. (Psalm 119:11)
As we reflect on our daily routine in the questions below, ponder the impact
scripture has had on your life, past and present.

Q1   With 1 Thessalonians 5:16-18 in mind, how do you remain in conversation with the Lord? Knowing that God is ever-present, do you consider Him when brewing a cup of coffee? As you sit down on the couch to put on your shoes, do you acknowledge Him? He is beside you right now as you read this. What does constant prayer look like in your daily routine?

_____

_____

_____

_____

_____

Q2   Nature walks, worship music, serving others... what moments in your day are ways that you would consider seeing God smile?

_____

_____

_____

_____

_____

Q3   If you wrote down every blessing throughout your day, you wouldn't be able to stop writing. And what about the unseen? We don't know everything that goes on behind the curtain. As you lay your head to rest each night, how do you show gratitude for immeasurable, exceeding abundance?

_____

_____

_____

_____

_____

Words Come

Come Lord, come. Speak into my life.

Your turn. Write your heart and mind.
Write a love letter to the Lord.

04.

Let Go

Divinely divide me, Lord.
Separate my flesh from my spirit and keep my spirit willing.
Division created by Your Word pierces my flesh and mends my soul.
It is necessary for Your Word to cut deep.
my flesh grips non essentials
that You, sadly, have to pry from me.
This is an act of love and fully necessary.
"Let go. This is pulling you away from Me."
There is a delicate manner in the way You
remove unhealthy ideas from me.
You don't snatch things out of my hands or my heart.
You wrap Your loving hand around my clenched fist emotions
and gently help me lift one finger at a time.
When the final finger is lifted,
an awareness emerges that clearly represents Your love.
Oh Lord, i see it.
Why was i gripping that so tightly?
It benefitted me none.
It was most certainly harming me.
Your heart is so tender.
You give me time.
You provide healing before You reveal the next expendable.

And there i go again . . . "wait Lord, not that one, i need that one."
"you don't child, you don't need this.
you have everything you need in Me."
There it goes . . . another idol turns to dust.
Disintegrated and swept away by the wind of
Your breath speaking truth over me.
Help me not to look back.
Keep going Lord, there are storehouses of unnecessary;
Egos, plans, false truths, selfish ambitions.
Illuminate and eliminate.
Remove what has no Kingdom value.
If You choose to hand me something, i won't grip it.
i will let it rest in the palm of my hand.
i won't play tug of war with You, should You decide to remove it.
i will simply trust that i no longer need it.
There is a comfort in being emptied out and refilled by You.
You are a purifying presence.
As You work, i see a familiar and similar beauty in our hands,
with one stand alone, significant difference.
No one will pry Your hand open and remove me from Your grip.
i am engraved on the palm of Your hand.
Gripped by God.

Scripture References
Matthew 26:41
Hebrews 4:12
2 Peter 3:9
John 7:37-38
John 10:27-30
Isaiah 49:16

Scripture Study & Questions

New believer or follower for many years, it is true the Holy Spirit speaks over lifestyle choices or habits that don't align with God's word or pull our focus away from Him. Let these questions penetrate your heart. Ask the Holy Spirit to join you in answering them.

Q1 How have you experienced the Holy Spirit revealing sin or convicting harmful habits? Do things need to be repeated several times? Do you find yourself making excuses or explaining your choices to God?

_____

_____

_____

_____

_____

Q2 2 Peter 3:9 describes God's patience with us. Share a specific time you have experienced the loving patience of God.

_____

_____

_____

_____

_____

Q3 John 10:27-30 is a reassurance that we are eternally held in God's hand. How does this promise give you peace? How does your heart respond?

_____

_____

_____

_____

_____

Words Come

05.

Posture

Is this what waiting looks like?
A bunch of question marks.
i am actually asking.
This isn't sarcasm.
i am seeking.
i ask with reverence, Lord.
i don't know what i am supposed to be doing.
i start something, "This is it!"
Until it isn't.
am i even supposed to feel discontentment?
It feels wrong to feel this longing.
my mind has so many ideas.
What do i do with all of these?
There are so many, i can't catalog them.
Just as i start to place one in a box, ten more arrive.
What is my job?
i am really asking.
am i already doing my job?
am i waiting for something that isn't on the way?
Anticipation and ambition are exhausting
Anticipation is met with expectation...great!
Why do i feel like i am still waiting?
Planning, striving, seeking, working,
i am tired, Lord.
So tired of chasing my brain.
i feel i am chasing an idea of myself,
that i created in my mind of how You want to see me.
am i "purpose" searching?
am i complicating simple?
Can a Christian have ambition?

Is this self-applied pressure?
Is the posture of my heart tilted?
This self-inflicted, pestering persistence to perform is futile.
And then there is the teeter-totter of emotions.
This constant fluctuating reflection invites motion sickness.
"How do i get off of this thing?"
Can You bring clarity to this perpetual confusion?
Breathe on this, Lord.
What doesn't belong will carry away in the breeze of Your Words.
The necessary will remain.
Truth grips.
It doesn't let go.
You don't let go.
You remain.
You are immoveable.
Renovate, reconcile, restore and rename.
Lengthen Your reach, Lord.
Surface cleansing isn't cleansing.
i don't want to be a white washed structure.
Step into these question marks.
Come Lord.
Put Your pen to my life and write my path.
Align my heart with Yours.
Purify motives.
Assign my life with Your truth.
Posture my heart with Your intended design.
i want the foundation of my heart to be You.
Start there.
Build everything around that.

Scripture References
James 4:1-3
2 Peter 1:10-11
1 Corinthians 12:12-31
1 Corinthians 7:17
Matthew 7:7
Matthew 23:27-28
Matthew 28:19-20
Philippians 1:6

Scripture Study & Questions

Have you ever had the perpetual childhood question, "what do you want to be when you grow up?" cycle into your adult life? Do you feel like you are always chasing an idea of yourself that your mind created? Does Christianity and ambition disagree? What does the phrase heart posture mean to you? Keep these questions in mind as you ponder the questions below.

Q1 Considering James 4:1-3, how do you continually evaluate the alignment of your heart posture to God's word?

_____
_____
_____
_____
_____

Q2 Paul encourages us to desire the greater gifts in 1 Corinthians 12. Have you ever asked God for one of these gifts? If so, which one and what thoughts arose leading to the desire for that particular gift?

_____
_____
_____
_____
_____

Q3 We all have God given gifts that stand out to others when they spend time with us. How do you employ your known strengths for the great commission?

_____
_____
_____
_____
_____

Words Come

06.

Tetelestai

I love you.

Telling you repeatedly wasn't enough.

I had to speak louder than words.

Sending My Son to you is giving you everything I've got.

Facing the judgement for your sin,

Innocence laid down His life for love.

Necessary for bringing you back to Me,

In Him alone,

Salvation and redemption are accomplished.

He conquered the grave,

Ending the sting of death.

Do you see how much you are loved?

Scripture Reference
John 3:16
Ephesians 1:7
Hosea 4:12
Ezekiel 18:30
Matthew 27:46
Psalm 22:1
1Corinthians 15:54-57

Scripture Study & Questions

The Old Testament is a clear example of God loving His creation and repeatedly reminding humanity to seek only Him. He is a good Father who over and over, shows mercy and desires to give good gifts. He provides, sustains, protects, relents and still humanity turns their back on Him.

Q1 If you consider that the Bible was written for us, not to us, how does the simplicity of the gospel truth embarrass the breadth of the Bible's stories of man's rebellion?

_____

_____

_____

_____

_____

Q2 What is your "go-to" gospel sharing statement for evangelism? Don't have one, write one. Practice on your small group or friends.

_____

_____

_____

_____

_____

Q3 The writing is written from the perspective of God talking to man. Considering John 3:16, how would you describe God's heart?

_____

_____

_____

_____

_____

Words Come

Consider using one of your words to write an acrostic poem like the writing.

07.

Secret Place

Seems more appropriate to say i am "in" prayer, rather than praying.
Prayer is a place i go, not something i do.
It isn't a structure, it doesn't have walls, yet it is a place where i arrive.
The earthly, physical realm seems to stand still.
The place of Prayer blankets my location like a soft dew covers the ground and our secret meeting location is revealed.
It isn't a dream.
It isn't a feeling.
It is a place.
You and i are the place.
We become the location.
Two worlds converge and share time.
Occupy all my time, Lord.
Share Your beautiful heart with me.
Graze my cheek with the smallest refraction of Your light.
And let me return, shiny.

Scripture Reference
Exodus 34:29-35
Deuteronomy 32:2
Zechariah 8:1-13

Scripture Study & Questions

I pray throughout the day and have morning and evening prayer time. Part of my prayer practice is getting on my knees several times a week, for at least a few moments in prayer. I ask God to accept my posture as reverent praise and worship. In those moments, I repeatedly say "thank You" and intentionally enter into a time of silence with an open heart and open ears. This posture is a personal choice. What is your prayer practice?

Q1 Have you ever considered prayer to be a place? What does the place look like? Detail what visually comes to your mind. If not a place, put into words, what secret time with the Lord looks like?

_____

_____

_____

_____

_____

Q2 Moses spent so much time with God, he returned to the community glowing. In 2 Corinthians 3:13-16, 18, Paul explains that the gospel truth of Jesus Christ allows us to live unveiled, shining always because of the glory of Christ inside us. How does prayer time with the Lord leave you feeling?

_____

_____

_____

_____

_____

Q3 What are some things that hinder or interrupt your attempt to enter into a secret prayer place with the Godhead? How do you combat those interruptions?

_____

_____

_____

_____

_____

Words Come

Praise Break

The wonderment in Your plan is far more captivating
than the shallow depth of my doubt.
i am going to wait in anticipation for a peek at
Your good and perfect will, should You lend me one.
i can be certain of Your intention.
Good.
Because i know who You are.
Love.
Your method invites curiosity.
Cancel confusion.
i'll remain confidently curious
and following the footprints You leave for me.
Be at work in me, Lord.
a gracious child of God, a servant heart,
a good steward of those You gift me,
and a life that bears fruit,
i offer myself to You freely.
Teach me.
Lead me.
Use me.

08.

Fellowship

Why do i put myself on a ledge?
Following You isn't always easy, but it is simple.
You are sure footing.
Stable and steady ground.
my feet slip on my own condemnation.
i can't imagine that pleases You.
Shame calling instead of name calling.
"Who taught you to talk to yourself that way?"
Scripture reflects conversations with Your creation
that sound nothing like the noise in my head.
Chase the chaos in my mind to very edge and breath on it.
These thoughts will fall to their deletion.
A Holy defense.
Cut down the hedge maze in my mind and lead me to thoughts of truth.
A Holy refocusing.
The longer i follow You, the shorter these spans of confusion last.
You are generous.
You send reinforcements.

Community comes and clarity arrives.
You have surrounded me with fellowship that sound a lot like You.
Their arrival is timely.
Imagine that . . . timeliness from You.
Seems to be a pattern of Yours,
delicate deliverance, spanning wisdom, and substantial support.
Clearly planted relationships connect me further to the Cornerstone.
Thank You for their overflow.
Source me to pour into others.
i want to respond in kind.
Community is a lovely companion.
Your intentional design creates cords of strength.
Using each other, to keep close to the Designer.
Image bearing agents of love, peace and hope
pointing back to the Original.
They are synonyms of You.
Your plan is plentiful and flawless.
You defined harmony in friendship.
Your gracious love and radiant light is abundant and beaming,
bouncing off my friends and landing on me.

Scripture Reference
Genesis 3:11
1Kings 19:12
James 1:5
Galatians 6:2
Ecclesiastes 4:12
Romans 8:28

Scripture Study & Questions

Island living wasn't the intended design. We learn in Genesis 2:18 through the appearance of Eve that God didn't intend for us to be alone. God is a good, loving Father giving us fellowship with Him and others through family, friendships, the church and complete strangers that we encounter in everyday life.

Q1   What does community look like to you? How do you connect with others?

_____

_____

_____

_____

_____

Q2   What prevents connection? Fears? Crowds? Status? Authenticity?

_____

_____

_____

_____

_____

Q3   What are tangible ways you can grow deeper relationships or expand your community by welcoming new ones? Life Group? Book Club? Volunteer Opportunities?

_____

_____

_____

_____

_____

Words Come

O9.

Heart Under Attack

There are edges to my heart.
i have a finite surface area for my emotions to explore.
Stable thoughts meet trying transitions and turn hard corners.
Shifting sides and sections can be jarring,
jumping from one emotional plain to the next.
i feel like i am dragging myself around my own heart.
Only i don't slow down long enough to steady a healthy cadence.
my beating heart has limits.
Boundaries.
Fear and anxiety increase the rate.
Rapid rhythms cause unrest.
Sadness signals intense pressure.
Heart under attack
I am not in pain, but i am in pain.

Put Your hand right here.
Do You feel it?
An overcrowded, dense space being further compressed.
Nothing else can be crammed in here, right now.
But then . . .
there is Your heart.
Your heart is a wide-open horizon with no end in sight.
Spanning plains of peace.
Stable and steady, unchanging rhythm.
Expansive surface of solace.
Synchronize our hearts.
Beat for beat, make mine sound like Yours.
Fuse my heart to Your heart, Lord.
Let the edges of my heart meet the eternity of Yours.

Scripture Reference
Romans 8:38-39
Ephesians 3:16-18
Psalm 103:8-12
Psalm 93:2

Scripture Study & Questions

The Bible states "His love endures forever" or a variation of this phrase 41 times. Scripture extensively and exhaustively displays the eternal love of God and His unchanging character. Our human hearts are limited and dependent upon His sustaining love. Let us consider for a moment, a side by side comparison of our fickle hearts to God's infinite spanning heart.

Q1 Describe Romans 8:38-39 in your own words. What attributes, characteristics and adjectives come to mind to describe the size of God's heart?

_____

_____

_____

_____

_____

Q2 Do you place pressure on yourself or try to be the "savior" for people in your community, rather than simply showing up and showing them the love of God through prayer and companionship? How can you be the hands and feet of Jesus, without trying to be the savior?

_____

_____

_____

_____

_____

Q3 Ever heard the statement; *you can't out sin God's love*? Are there people in your life who call themselves Christians, but live like God's love is a freedom to live any way they want? How can you exemplify God's love and grace for them with the kindness of truth?

_____

_____

_____

_____

_____

Words Come

10.

Potter

In Your hands Lord.
That is where i want to be.
You gently mend my chipped edges.
You carefully repair the cracks of my heart.
i am a dusty clay vessel in the hands of the Potter.
The beauty in Your work are the indentions
Your hands leave behind.
Visible thumb prints evident of the Creator's presence.
Your restorative work lends a glimpse of previous breaks.
You turn fractures into art.
"Do you see this scar?"
i share my healed wounds.
"See, right here, He put these pieces back together
and made me whole."

Lord, i want to share the stories behind my scars,
the way Your flawless work works on my flawed choices.
You are the Original Artisan.
my Lord, i am Yours.
i am only useful in Your hands.
Fill me with Your life-giving water and pour me out onto others.
i want to share like You do.
You give so freely of Yourself.
Teach me to give like that.
i would rather be a cracked clay pot in Your hands,
than the polished, glazed vanity i see in the world.
Pick me up Lord.
In Your hands, is where i want to be.
Useful.

Scripture Reference
Isaiah 64:8
John 7:38
Philippians 2:17
Ephesians 6:19-20
Romans 8:32

Scripture Study & Questions

God is our source for everything, and we can be useful for His Kingdom when we are in His hands. He can and does use us for drawing others closer to Him. Let's discuss how being in the hands of the Potter grows our faith, confirms our purpose in His perfect will and keeps us close to our Source of life.

Q1 Read Isaiah 49:16. What thoughts or emotions come to mind when you ponder being engraved on the palm of God's hand?

_____

_____

_____

_____

_____

Q2 We all have scars from either being hurt or being the one who did the hurting. When you consider Paul's previous life as Saul and his later statement of being "in chains for Christ", how you do think he viewed his emotional scars?

_____

_____

_____

_____

_____

Q3 Romans 8:32 is one of many scriptures telling us that God freely gives. How can you present your scars to freely give for the sake of others and the Kingdom?

_____

_____

_____

_____

_____

Words Come

11.

Lies

Panic set in this morning.
A lovely addition to the doubt i swam in yesterday.
In a twenty-four hour period,
a mental Olympic Games has taken place.
And my head was the arena they were played in.
The orchestra of lies i was fed put my heart in critical care.
Do my prayers have prying ears?
What began as gentle conviction, disguised as light
became painful, penetrating questions that felt like blows.
Hit after hit, i quickly recognized the intruder.
Here they come. . .
"you think He finds you useful?"
"you think He hears anything you say?"
"you are just noise, in a sea of noise."
"you are self-seeking, not Kingdom serving."
"Keep calling Him, go ahead. . .
That's funny, i don't hear any response."

i called You, Lord, i know You heard me.
I called You again and again.
i know You have every single tear in a jar with my name on it.
i fought back but, felt puny.
i perceived distance between us.
Another lie.
An awfully noisy, thorny nuisance he is.
i felt the heat of trial and a wave of torment.
A soft sweet reminder pierced the darkness.
Now i sit in the warmth of Your counseling embrace.
Thank You for answering the actual questions i asked,
And, for refuting his testimony about me.
his words most certainly do return void.
Your Word stands forever.
his attempts to slay my faith,
confirm that You are my every need fulfilled.
You increase the depth and breadth of my belief.
Healer of my unbelief,
When You seem quiet,
i will hold fast to the words You have already spoken.
i will abide.

Scripture Reference
Psalm 56:8
2 Corinthians 12:7-10
Isaiah 55:11
Job 13:15
Mark 9:24

Scripture Study & Questions

Deception is a darkness the enemy uses to cloud our minds with confusion. We learn from scripture that Satan is the Father of lies. (John 8:44) But Jesus is the author and perfecter of our faith. (Hebrews 12:2) The Devil is a created being. He is limited. Though our reach is also limited, we are connected to a limitless power that also happens to love us inexplicably.

Q1 What does a trip through your mind look like? What would someone find? Scripture? Contentment? Compartments? Judgement? Self-deprecation?

_____

_____

_____

_____

_____

Q2 If the enemy's tactics are confusion and lies, how do you fight back with the truth? What practices do you have in place that bring you out of a cycle of confusion?

_____

_____

_____

_____

_____

Q3 When considering the thorn in Paul's flesh, how does his application of plugging his weakness into the One, true source of power give you confidence in the weakness of your flesh and against enemy arrows?

_____

_____

_____

_____

_____

Words Come

12.

Saints

Slowly, lowly,
i decrease Lord.
When i race to the humility line,
i boast in my speed.
No, it can't be that way.
i don't want to harm humility with my entrance.
Just gently open the door and sit in the back.
Listen intently to those already in the room.
their grace is sweet.
their action is informed and deliberate.
Needed and timely.
they look like You, Lord.
A room full of Saints.
Within just a few feet of them,
i can hear their hearts singing Your praise.
they beam.
Sitting near them is warmth.

It is obvious they spend time with You.
their compassion is considerable.
Which is how i think they got here.
Spending time with You makes people look like this.
they're beauty draws me in.
Hearts fully on display, i see beauty's definition.
Splendid lights of Christ everywhere i look.
Let me simply say thank You for them.
they are teaching me what You taught them.
Come closer, Lord, get even closer.
And here You are.
The Lord is in this place.
The King is among His people.
The humble servant King is still teaching.
Give me ears to hear.
Teach good Teacher.

Scripture Reference
2 Corinthians 3:18
Ephesians Ch 4
Proverbs 15:22
1 Peter 2:9

Scripture Study & Questions

Saints, Disciples, the Hall of Faith from Hebrews; what emotions come to mind when you read or hear these terms? Ponder the power source behind these giants of faith in scripture, their courage, fear, emotions and reward.

Q1   How would you characterize your walk with Jesus? Your faith? Are you a new believer, just born again? Are you a lifelong follower of Christ? Would you refer to yourself as a Saint? Why or Why not?

_____

_____

_____

_____

_____

Q2   What does being a disciple of Jesus Christ mean to you?

_____

_____

_____

_____

_____

Q3   Do you have a Paul who pours into you? Do you have a Timothy you pour into? Elaborate on these relationships and what impact they have had in your life.

_____

_____

_____

_____

_____

Words Come

13.

Antidote

No more.
i don't want to be fearful of this world.
i want to be fierce for the Kingdom.
Anxiety flees worship of the Lord.
Lift praise, take flight.
Carry my words to Heaven.
i am fighting back.
But i don't fight alone.
i walk in the footsteps of the Almighty God.
i step where He steps.
He sets the pace and i simply follow.
Fleeting world,
you have nothing to offer me.
my praise belongs to the Most High.
Failure turns to valor when Light leads the way.
My eyes are fixed on the light of Jesus Christ.
Falling down doesn't hurt any longer.

Stumbling becomes strength and becomes sure footing.
See, it's a Rock that i stand on.
The Founder of foundation.
The Original always.
The always existing Rock that created the ages.
Run from me worry, run away.
Be wary worry, i have found your weakness.
The antidote to your poison lives inside me.
He flows through my veins.
i have a superweapon.
He sharpens my mind and makes my heart battle ready.
i have become acutely aware of the schemes around me.
i am dialed in and armed with righteous words.
my senses are attuned to His perfect will.
i have only one thing to do today . . .
Follow Him.
Lead on, Jesus.
i am right behind You.

Scripture Reference
Exodus 14:14
Ephesians 6:10-17
1 Corinthians 16:13-14
Psalm 118:6-7
Romans 8:11

Scripture Study & Questions

We follow the only real superhero that eternity exists. Oh, and bonus, the Spirit of that superhero lives inside those who believe in Him. The Holy Spirit is the eternal existing power that brought Jesus back to life. This information can and should increase your heart rate, activate senses you didn't know existed and soar your confidence in sharing the truth.
Remember Who you fight for and Who fights for you.

Q1 Exact same power! Not a duplicate or a copy. The more times something is copied, the weaker the copies get. You don't have a copy of the Holy Spirit. You have the Original living inside you. What words come to mind, knowing this truth.

_____
_____
_____
_____
_____

Q2 Fierce not fear. How can the scriptures we have examined make you battle ready and unafraid?

_____
_____
_____
_____
_____

Q3 Have you ever closed your eyes and visually imagined putting on the armor of God? Consider this impenetrable, invisible armor sealed by the Holy Spirit covering your body. How can you encourage and equip others to join you and suit up?

_____
_____
_____
_____
_____

Words Come

14.

Awaken

Wake up sleeper.
Arrest this slumber.
There is work to do.
you have been called and consecrated.
Blessed are the ignited,
initiated and intentional.
Recognize Who calls you to action,
The sweet Sovereign.
Blessed are the purposeful,
pioneered by peace.
Internally empowered,
Counselor indwelled, arise.
Blessed are the appointed anointed,
awaken and activate.
Recognize your mission.
Respond with action.
Wield the Word of Truth.
Christian, share your Namesake.
Prophesy won't be prolonged.
Don't confuse His patience with your delay.
Blessed are the obedient,
Kingdom driven, sharing saints.
Christ follower, portion the inheritance.
Don't keep it to yourself.
Wake up sleeper.
There is work to do.
Begin.

Scripture Reference
Matthew 28:19-20
Matthew 5:3-12
Luke 24:46-49
Acts 1:8
Habakkuk 2:3
Matthew 24:14

Scripture Study & Questions

God's plan will not be thwarted, and Jesus' return is imminent. As stated in Matthew 24:36, we do not know the day or hour, so we live in anticipation and under the commission of Jesus to "go".

Q1 Do you see gaps of downtime or moments of pause in your life as a Christ follower? Have there been periods of ignition and action or periods of delay or resistance?
How do we stay consistent in our walk and finish the race?

_____

_____

_____

_____

_____

Q2 Have you ever considered Jesus's return in respect to the timeline of your own life? Hopefully you call Jesus your Savior and if so, how does His tarry overwhelm you with gratitude?

_____

_____

_____

_____

_____

Q3 Consider the people in your everyday life and even the strangers that you encounter in a week. How many don't know the love of Jesus Christ? Contemplating the gratitude you have as a believer, how does the truth of the gospel ignite a desire to share with others, knowing that God is patient, not wanting even one to perish?

_____

_____

_____

_____

_____

Words Come

15.

Hallel

Hallel.
Maranatha.
Hear my words.
Accept them as worship.
i am content, my Lord.
i can't reach a level of praise worthy of the way Your encompassing
love makes me feel.
i can't reach an emotional altitude anywhere near
the gratitude Your goodness deserves.
i kneel and squint with my eyes and my heart in praise.
With all my might, though small and slight, i love You.
Selah
You are availably near.
You are on my left and my right.
You are in and surrounding.
You are surface and deep.
Closer than my next breath.

Inhale, God is my Father.
Exhale, release the world.
Inhale, in Jesus' name.
Exhale, tension and anxiety.
Selah
Your love is exquisite, radiant and whole.
Your love isn't brief or subtle.
Come closer.
No, Lord, even closer.
Draw near to Your servant.
i am sincerely Yours and earnestly gripping Your steadfast love.
Look in my direction, Lord.
Lend me just a glance.
A moment, just a moment with You is enduring.
Ever linger, Lord.

Scripture Reference
1 Thessalonians 5:16-18
Philippians 4:11-13
Isaiah 30:21
Hebrews 1:3
Matthew 11:28-30

Scripture Study & Questions

As you have probably discovered from a brief internet search, Aramaic & Hebrew words were chosen to express praise and closeness to God in this writing. The word Selah is used in Psalms and Habakkuk to identify a deliberate pause for reflection. Words can be beautiful and give life, or they can tear down and destroy. Reflect on how your praise to God can lift you, force the enemy to flee and encourage those around you.

Q1 List 5 words or phrases that come to mind when you think of praise and worship.

_____

_____

_____

_____

_____

Q2 If you remember anything from this study, let it be that anxiety and fear flee worship of the Lord. What is your praise practice? How will you fight back when fear arrives?

_____

_____

_____

_____

_____

Q3 How has your relationship with God, your connection to scripture, or word choices changed during this study?

_____

_____

_____

_____

_____

Words Come

40, 66, 1189
1

A Wandering
Through the Word

Let there be light.
In the beginning was the Word, and the Word was with God,
and the Word was God.
He was with God in the beginning.
Through Him all things were made;
without Him nothing was made that has been made.
In Him was life, and that life was the light of all mankind.
The light shines in the darkness, and the darkness has not overcome it.
The true light that gives light to everyone was coming into the world.
The Word became flesh and made his dwelling among us.
We have seen His glory, the glory of the one and only Son,
who came from the Father, full of grace and truth.
Every good and perfect gift is from above,
coming down from the Father of heavenly lights,
who does not change like shifting shadows.
The Son is the radiance of God's glory
and the exact representation of His being,
sustaining all things by His powerful word.
The unfolding of Your words gives light;
Your Word is a lamp for my feet, a light on my path.
Hold firmly to the word of life.
For the Word of God is alive and active.
Whoever has ears to hear, let them hear.
I am the light of the world.
Whoever follows me will never walk in darkness,
but will have the light of life.
Remain in me, as I also remain in you.
Remain in my love.
My command is this: Love each other as I have loved you.

I am the good shepherd.

My sheep listen to my voice; I know them, and they follow me.

I give them eternal life, and they shall never perish;

no one will snatch them out of my hand.

My Father, who has given them to me, is greater than all;

no one can snatch them out of my Father's hand.

I and the Father are one.

If you love me, keep my commands.

And I will ask the Father,

and He will give you another advocate to help you

and be with you forever-the Spirit of Truth.

But the Advocate, the Holy Spirit, whom the Father will send

in My name, will teach you all things

and will remind you of everything I have said to you.

He will guide you into all the truth.

He will not speak on His own;

He will speak only what He hears,

and He will tell you what is yet to come.

He will glorify me because it is from me

that He will receive what He will make known to you.

All that belongs to the Father is Mine.

Peace I leave with you;

My Peace I give you.

Do not be afraid.

I am the good Shepherd.

The good shepherd lays down his life for the sheep.

No one takes it from me, but I lay it down of my own accord.

Father, the hour has come.

Glorify Your Son, that Your Son may glorify You.

For You granted Him authority over all people that
He might give eternal life to all those You have given Him.
Now this is eternal life: that they know You,
the only true God, and Jesus Christ, whom You have sent.
I have brought You glory on earth
by finishing the work you gave me to do.
Holy Father, protect them by the power of Your name,
the name You gave me, so that they may be one as we are one.
I am coming to You now, but I say these things while I am still in the
world, so that they may have the full measure of My joy within them.
My prayer is not for them alone.
I pray also for those who will believe in Me through their message, that
all of them may be one, Father, just as You are in Me and I am in You.
May they also be in us.
My Father, if it is possible, may this cup be taken from me.
Yet, not as I will, but as you will.
Look, the hour has come, and the Son of Man
is delivered into the hands of sinners.
It is finished.
With a loud cry, Jesus breathed His last.
The curtain of the temple was torn in two from top to bottom.
He was pierced for our transgressions,
He was crushed for our iniquities;
the punishment that brought us peace was on Him,
and by His wounds we are healed.
"He himself bore our sins" in His body on the cross,
so that we might die to sins and live for righteousness.
For the transgression of my people he was punished.

Why do you look for the living among the dead?
You are looking for Jesus the Nazarene, who was crucified.
He has risen!
He is not here.
Who shall separate us from the love of Christ?
For I am convinced that neither death nor life, neither angels nor
demons, neither the present nor the future, nor any powers, neither
height nor depth, nor anything else in all creation, will be able to
separate us from the love of God that is in Christ Jesus our Lord.
I have been crucified with Christ and I no longer live,
but Christ lives in me.
The life I now live in the body, I live by faith in the Son of God,
who loved me and gave Himself for me.
For to me, to live is Christ and to die is gain.
Let us run with perseverance the race marked out for us,
fixing our eyes on Jesus, the pioneer and perfecter of faith.
For the joy set before Him He endured the cross,
scorning its shame, and sat down at the right hand of the throne of God.
Now to Him who is able to do immeasurably
more than all we ask or imagine,
according to His power that is at work within us,
to Him be the glory in the church and in Christ Jesus
throughout all generations for ever and ever!
Amen.

The Son is the image of the invisible God, the firstborn over all creation. For in Him, all things were created; things in heaven and on earth, visible and invisible, whether thrones or power or rulers or authorities; all things have been created through Him and for Him. He is before all things and in Him all things hold together. And He is the head of the body, the church; He is the beginning and the firstborn from among the dead, so that in everything He might have the supremacy. For God was pleased to have all His fullness dwell in Him, and through Him to reconcile to himself all things, whether things on earth or things in heaven, by making peace through His blood, shed on the cross. Once you were alienated from God and were enemies in your minds because of evil behavior. But now He has reconciled you by Christ's physical body through death to present you holy in His sight, without blemish and free from accusation.

Colossians 1:15-22

Heaven is on the horizon.

www.ingramcontent.com/pod-product-compliance
Lightning Source LLC
Chambersburg PA
CBHW041537120626
46551CB00019B/2731